the Book of Cups

the Book of Cups

Garth Clark

Photography by Tony Cunha

Abbeville Press · Publishers · New York · London · Paris

Editor: Constance Herndon
Designer: Molly Shields
Production editor: Laura Lindgren
Production director: Dana Cole

Library of Congress Cataloging-in-Publication Data
Clark, Garth, 1947–
The book of cups
1. Drinking cups—History.   2. Pottery—History   3. Porcelain—History.   I. Title
NK 4695.C8C54   1990   738   89-18211
ISBN 0-7892-0170-4

First paperback edition
2 4 6 8 10 9 7 5 3 1

Page 1: Late nineteenth-century die-cut sticker or stamp manufactured in England.
Frontispiece: Detail from a late nineteenth-century tea advertisement.
Title page: Kasuye Sueymatsu, *Mermaid Cup and Saucer*, 1980. Porcelain, 3½ in. high.
Below: James Lawton, *Cup and Saucer*, 1983. Raku-fired earthenware, 4¾ in. high.
Front cover: center, see page 56; clockwise from
top right, see pages 89, 21, 51, 15, 42, 76.
Back flap: Don Schreckengost, Salem Pottery,
Tricorne Cup, c. 1940. Ceramic, 3¼ in. high.
Back cover: see page 32.

Contents

Foreword

I was only seven years old when I formally met my first cup. It was at this tender age that my parents served me a cup of tea in their best china, and with no bidding my small finger curled back in the manner of the formal tea. I am still not sure whether this reflexive action was the result of some precognitive sense of form or a mis-wiring of the tendons in my hand, but it still happens whenever I pick up a cup. While my parents were mildly amused by my precociously affected digit, this was a sign to me that the teacup and I were to enjoy a special relationship.

This has indeed been the case. As both a lover of tea and an historian of ceramics (and more lately a

Philip Guston
Cup, *1972*
Oil on masonite, 12 × 14 in.

Philip Guston

7

Betty Asher and a few of her cups.

dealer) I have found that the cup has loomed sur-
prisingly large in my life, given its modest scale. I have
written articles and curated exhibitions about the cup,
lectured on its charms, and published a book about its
matriarch, the teapot. At one point I even decided to
make cups myself, and although I did learn to throw
and produced a passable set of mugs, this brief odys-
sey into the wet and plastic world of raw clay left me
convinced that my interest in ceramics was definitely in
the drier, tidier world of connoisseurship.

My education into the art of the cup was greatly
enhanced in 1981 when I met Betty Asher. She was
already something of a legend by then, her cups having
collectively and individually appeared in countless
exhibitions throughout the United States and abroad.
For thirteen years, until 1979, she had also worked as
the assistant to Maurice Tuchman, curator of modern
art at the Los Angeles County Museum of Art,
resigning to open the Asher/Faure Gallery in Los
Angeles with Patty Faure. The gallery was soon
established as one of the premier venues for contemporary art on the West Coast.

Asher drives a convertible with the license plate
CUPS, which is warning enough that this is no minor
passion. She has collected cups since the 1960s when
she first acquired works by the artist Kenneth Price,

who in turn introduced her to a disciple and fellow cup-maker Ron Nagle, and the interest was born. In 1985 the remarkable quality of her collection was recognized when the Los Angeles County Museum acquired eighty-six of her cups, which have been kept on permanent display in the new Robert O. Anderson wing of the museum alongside other masterpieces of twentieth-century art.

From the outset Asher's interest has been in the cup as an expression of creativity. She admits with just a shade of embarrassment that she is not a tea drinker, and that the utilitarian aspects of the cup hold little fascination for her. Instead her collection has focused on the idea of the cup as the departure point to the more quirky, irrational, and eccentric edges of human expression.

Moreover Asher sees the cup as an image and does not restrict herself to the cup's conventional three dimensions. Her collection includes cup-related jewelry, clothing, rubber stamps, postcards, die-stamped and cup-shaped advertisements, paintings, prints, drawings, photography, and even refrigerator magnets. What makes the collection exciting is its egalitarian mixture of fine art, decorative art, and found objects. In her spacious Los Angeles home, a cracked and peeling café sign shares wall space with a

As the legend on the back of this early sixties postcard of a Tempe, Arizona, amusement park declares, "The unpredictable Krazy Kups are a rollicking breathtaking adventure in the fabulous modern amusement section of this magnificent Family Fun Park."

Cup and Saucer Bank,
c. 1920
Brass, 4½ in. high

masterful painting by Philip Guston. Cups acquired
for fifty cents at garage sales sit alongside unique cup
sculptures by Pop artists Claes Oldenburg and Roy
Lichtenstein. Unified by a common format and
Asher's perceptive collecting "eye," these diverse objects emerge as equals, shunning the conventional pol-
itics of high and low art.

As in all successful collections, this diverse assem-
bly of works reflects the personality of the collector.
Characterized by an adventurous openness (Asher
was one of the first in Los Angeles to acquire the

Linda Hesh
Just My Cup of Tea, *1984*
Silver, 3 in. high

*A drawer from Betty Asher's
jewelry cabinet.*

13

Un bonjour et à votre santé!
Vive la bonne tasse de Huy

works of Warhol, Lichtenstein, Oldenburg, Johns, and Ruscha), this collection has an aura of youthfulness that has nothing to do with chronology. Asher's dry wit provides a unifying focus for this amalgam of cups. Few of the objects are merely eccentric for eccentricity's sake; most provide an underlying commentary about the human condition and the culture in

French postcard from the 1920s.

which it exists. But the central idea is that of the cup as a transformative device—as a product of an untrammeled imagination.

Asher's focus and her choices have shaped this book. Because her collection focuses on contemporary cups rather than on those of the past, I have included a few historical cups from public institutions in order to illustrate the text and explain precedent. I have also "infiltrated" her collection with a few modern cups in private hands to exemplify certain ideas and styles.

This book, however, is not intended to be an academic study but a celebration of the lowly but essential cup. After all, Betty Asher has never been an academic collector. She has acquired intuitively for pleasure. In the process she has obtained a body of small twentieth-century masterpieces by painters, sculptors, and ceramists as well as a fascinating group of less revered, but no less revealing, cultural artifacts.

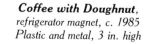

Coffee with Doughnut,
refrigerator magnet, c. 1985
Plastic and metal, 3 in. high

Marilyn Lysohir
**Dazzle Cup and Saucer with
Ship**, *1986*
Ceramic, 3½ in. high

The Book of Cups

The cup is the drone of the ceramics world, perhaps the hardest working of vessels and the least appreciated. In the grandest of tea or coffee services, the cup is usually the most underdesigned object, playing the role of subservient pawn to the teapot's queen. But this book is not about passively utilitarian cups—these are cups of invention and adventure.

History has not been particularly fair to the cup. While vases, urns, and teapots have been extolled by poets, painters, and musicians, there has been, for instance, no "Ode on a Grecian Cup." It appears to be a quirk of human nature that we take for granted those objects (and indeed people) that are most useful.

Anonymous photograph from the fifties.

Anna Silver
Cup, 1989
Glazed and painted whiteware,
2 in. high

Moreover the cup does not have any immediate sense of drama—it is small and comprised of at most two elements, a vessel and usually a handle. But that does not mean the drama is absent, rather that we need to examine the cup a little more closely and consciously to discover its sense of domestic theater.

While we have not celebrated the cup in the same way as we have the Greek vase or the Sung bowl, it has nonetheless entered our collective consciousness

Tom Rippon
Nostalgia, 1984
Porcelain, 6 × 8 in.

Barbara Spring
Large Cup of Cocoa, *1989,*
Small Cup of Cocoa and
Marshmallow, *1987,*
Stacked Cups, *1989*
Wood, 3 to 5½ in. high

through language and metaphor. A small but over-blown crisis is referred to as a "tempest in a teacup." "Many a slip twixt cup and lip" speaks volumes about oral contracts made over coffee and tea. The Bible says that "our cup runneth over" when we have been generously blessed in some way. If someone is said to be "in his cups" we know that he has imbibed too much alcohol. On the other hand, "just his cup of tea" refers to a perfect match.

The Cup Exalted: A Revisionist History

Still, the cup is more than a metaphor; indeed its history is as complex as any of the applied arts. No one knows exactly when men and women fashioned the first cups. But it was a momentous day when our hirsute primeval ancestors discovered that instead of plunging their heads into streams they could bring water to their mouths in the cups of their hands. Later, cups were improvised from leaves and gourds. About eight thousand years ago men and women learned that clay placed into fire would harden and could hold liquids. At that point the ceramic cup as we know it today began to emerge, reaching its stylish *belle époch* in the court porcelains of the eighteenth century.

Eric Zammitt
Untitled, 1984
Bark, 3¼ in. high

Native American
Cup Miniatures, *c. 1970*
Ceramic, ⅞ in. high

Native American
Cups, *c. 1950*
Fiber, 3 and 2¾ in. high

23

The cups and mugs in this collection are mainly Western examples of handled drinking vessels rather than Far Eastern bowl models. Unlike the teapot, which is a mere four hundred years old, the handled cup as we know it today is at least three thousand years old. Mycenaeans living in Cyprus in 1100 B.C. drank from cups that have exactly the same form as modern cup designs. Even earlier examples made of metal existed around 1000 B.C. in the Minoan culture. Then as now, potters made miniature cups as playthings for children and as novelty items.

The ancient Greeks took the cups of Mycenaean and Minoan cultures and gave them a classical grandeur. A popular form, the cup even attracted its own specialist painters who used it as their personal canvas. Elaborately painted "parade" cups (frequently showing languidly sexual scenes of Dionysian revelry) were made for the symposium drinking parties that were a traditional part of Greek recreation.

These Greek cups took several forms, from the rare, single-handled kythasos to the double-handled, thick-walled skyphos. But a form called the kylix is one of the most dazzling marvels of classical refinement. These two-handled cups originating around 500 B.C. are characterized by a delicate saucer-shaped vessel on an elegant pedestal foot. With its

Greek-Attic
Kylix, *c. 510–500* B.C.
Red figure earthenware,
3³/₁₆ in. high
The Metropolitan Museum of Art,
New York, Fletcher Fund, 1956

sublime sense of contour and silhouette, the kylix is a perfect example of the Greek potter's concept of dynamic symmetry. Around 700 B.C. in Corinth these cups began to be decorated with black figures against a reddish terra-cotta ground, followed around 530 B.C. by red figure painting (red figures against a black ground), which dominated Greek pottery for a thousand years.

Not only did the kylix establish an esthetic standard but its very form prescribed graceful behavior, for its extremely shallow shape demanded a steady hand—unlike the medieval tankard, which, with its tall body

and narrow mouth, was ideally suited for slopping ale into even the most inebriated tavern brawler. Greeks served a watered wine at their parties, the exact proportions of whose two ingredients was the source of endless philosophical debate and, no doubt, some intoxicatingly practical experimentation.

The kylix when used for drinking was held at the bottom of the cup. The main purpose of its handles was to hang up the cup after use. Because the kylix was stored in this way, its undersides were extensively painted so that they would look suitably decorative on the wall. In certain paintings on Greek pots, however, we see the kylix being held with a finger through one handle, the manner in which the cup was held for a game called *kottabos*, which involved tossing the dregs of wine at a lamp stand with the objective of knocking over the lamp's decorative finial.

In the otherwise pure and classical world of the Greek potter, certain elements appeared of what might be termed "novelty." A bawdy kylix in the collection of the Ashmolean Museum, Oxford, has a satyr mask inside and modeled male genitals as the foot. Some rare cups with sphinx feet exist, and some amphoras are painted with even more fantastic cups, which were either simply the product of the painter's imagination or are pieces that have been lost to history.

Ingeborg Strobl
Hoof Pitcher with Cup,
1972–73
Earthenware, 2¾ and 8 in. high
Private collection

*Card advertising Mazawattee brand
tea, c. 1906.*

British, Staffordshire
Fox and Hound Hunt Cups,
c. 1750–1825
Ceramic, 5 and 5⅛ in. high
Everson Museum of Art, Syracuse,
New York, Gift of Joseph Caldwell

Greek-Athenian
**Rhyton in Form of Ram's
Head**, *c. 550* B.C.
*Red figure earthenware,
4½ in. high
The Metropolitan Museum of Art,
New York, Fletcher Fund, 1939*

The Greeks also produced unusual cups known as rhytons—Eastern inspired, footless, religious offering cups in the form of an animal's head. Another variant of this idea was the mastos, a breast-shaped cup with a nipple base.

Tygs, Frogs, and Puzzles: Medieval and Renaissance Cups

Although the cup became an object of great invention in the hands of the ancient Greeks, in the following centuries this lowly little object sank back into design oblivion—indeed not until the late medieval and early modern periods in Britain did the cup again begin to evolve. Of course the style of the medieval period was very different from that of Greece. Life was cruder and less well mannered, and the drinking vessels express this condition: they are sturdy, rough objects, but their raciness and rustic beauty place these late medieval slipwares among the finest and most honest pottery ever made.

Unlike the watered wine favored by the Greeks, the favorite beverage of this period was an unpleasant-sounding brew known as posset, a hot drink concocted from sweetened milk that was curdled with wine or ale. The lumpy liquid was either sucked through the

Advertising card from the 1920s portraying a gleefully self-destructive sugar cube.

David Pendell (left) and John Reveley (right)
Mr. Peanut's Commentary on Society, *1985,*
and **Mr. Peanut,** *1972*
Ceramic, 3¾ in. high

spout of a lidded posset pot or drunk from a posset cup
or tyg. The latter was a communal cup that had
several handles so it could easily be grasped from all
sides of the table. In the late seventeenth and early
eighteenth centuries these cups reached their decorative apex, primitively but elaborately decorated
with painted, trailed, and feathered slips under a
galena or lead glaze.

Another specialty of the medieval potter was the
two-handled "loving cup," so named because it was
made for weddings. The cup would be passed around
the table to toast the bride and groom, whose names

British
Two-handled Cup, *18th century*
Ceramic, 5¼ in. high
The Metropolitan Museum of Art,
New York, Rogers Fund, 1912

The comforts of the cup—late 19th
century painting depicting the simple
pleasures of a warm cup of tea.

British, Staffordshire
Posset Pot, *1759*
White slip on red earthenware,
7¼ in. high
Nelson-Atkins Museum of Art,
Kansas City

Tom Otterness
Cup and Spoon, *1986*
Cast bronze, 6¼ in. high

David Gilhooly
Hot Chocolate, *1986*
Earthenware, 4½ in. high

David Gilhooly
Cream in Your Coffee, *1987*
Plastic, 4½ in. high

would often be drawn in slip on the surface of the cup by the potter.

In the cockeyed spirit of the inebriates their cups usually held, medieval potters developed a number of novelty tavern cups. Their humor was simple: one of the most popular of these was the frog mug, in which a small modeled frog was placed at bottom to emerge just as unsuspecting drinkers quaffed the last swallow of ale. This mug has recently been revived in English pottery as a popular novelty item. The frog mug finds its most madcap expression in the fecund frog world of

Marilyn Lysohir
Cup with Chocolates and Deviled Eggs, *1984*
Earthenware, 4³⁄4 in. high

Robert Arneson
Rock Cup, 1974
Earthenware, 5 in. high

Mike Johns
Rock Cup, 1987
*Earthenware with low-fire glaze and
luster, 5 in. high*

Rachel Todd
Satyns Cup, 1988
Ceramic, 3½ in. high

Mexican
Cups, *1930s*
Ceramic, 2¾ to 3½ in. high

Edward Weston
Hot Coffee, Mohave Desert,
1937
Silver print photograph,
7⅜ × 9⅜ in.

ceramist David Gilhooly, whose amphibians do not lie demurely submersed but blithely cavort in a cup of chocolate that has become their swimming pool, complete with marshmallows for pool toys.

Puzzle mugs were also popular between the sixteenth and eighteenth centuries. The puzzle mug sabotages the drinker with an internal "plumbing" system that can feed into a number of holes on the lip (and sometimes in the handle). The trick is to suck at the right hole while keeping the right number of other holes closed with one's fingers. Fuddling mugs, intercon-

George E. Ohr
Puzzle Mug, *c. 1900*
Earthenware, 3½ in. high
To drink from this mug one had to suck through the correct hole while keeping certain others covered. It derives from a tradition of medieval tavern joke mugs.

Christopher Gustin
Red Cup and Saucer, *1988*
Stoneware, 5 in. high

George E. Ohr
Three Mugs, *c. 1900*
Earthenware, 4 to 5 in. high

nected groups of three, four, or five mugs, were an elaboration of this. To avoid being doused in ale, one had to drink from these in precisely the correct order. The occasional puzzle mug is still made today, but they are complex objects and the last important body of these gimcracks was produced at the turn of the century by maverick potter George E. Ohr. A tireless prankster and punster, Ohr recreated a good number of these entertaining objects.

Porcelain and the Pompous Cup

In the eighteenth century the curdled charms of posset gave way to more delicate brews as the British lifestyle began to change. The island nation was now fast becoming a land of coffee, tea, and chocolate drinkers, a situation that required elegant cups rather than the rough peasant wares of the British slipware maker. In the late seventeenth and early eighteenth centuries, before the handled teacup was developed, the upper classes used expensive "export ware" porcelain tea bowls and saucers from China. Only nobility could afford these extremely costly cups. Ownership of a porcelain cup indicated a high social station, and it was very common for the nobility to pose for portraits holding their favorite cup and saucer. Indeed the teacup or bowl was considered so important and so

Russian, St. Petersburg
Cup and Saucer with Monogram of Czarina Alexandra, *early twentieth century*
Porcelain, 2¾ in. high
The Metropolitan Museum of Art, New York, Gift of R. Thornton Wilson, 1950, in memory of Florence Ellsworth Wilson

Anne Kraus
Cup and Saucer with Teapot,
1983
Glazed whiteware, 2¾ in. high

Anne Kraus
Lovers' Cup, *1984*
Earthenware, 4 in. high

I ACHED TO
SUDDENLY REALIZE
THE WORLDS THAT
SEPARATE US

personal that it was customary for one to carry one's own to tea parties in a special leather-and-satin carrying case.

In 1709 Germany's Miessen Porcelain Works began to produce the first true European porcelains. Up until this time the porcelain formula had evaded Western potters despite energetic attempts to discover its secret. But the domestic production of porcelain in Europe did not immediately make these wares more affordable, for porcelain factories were run as royal monopolies to serve the wealthy. While their elaborate

Turner of Lane's End
Prince of Orange Cup and Saucer, *1770–90*
Creamware, 1⅝ in. high
Everson Museum of Art, Syracuse, New York, Gift of Cynthia B. and Benjamin J. Lake

wares remained costly and greatly coveted, however, they did influence design, inspiring a new delicacy and opulence in Western ceramics.

Not until the eighteenth century did the handled cup and the saucer gain popularity. Legend has it that this design was introduced and popularized by the Marquise de Pompadour, an assertion hotly contested by some historians. Although the Greeks had used a saucer or cup "stand" over two thousand years earlier, the saucer came to the West from China, evolving from the bowl and stand, a ritualized form for displaying vessels in the Far East. The early European saucer was designed with a deep bowl-like shape so that tea could be poured into the saucer to cool (some philistines even slurped their tea directly from the saucer).

Griffen, Smith, and Hill
**Shell and Seaweed Cup and
Saucer**, *1880–90*
*Glazed earthenware, 2¼ in. high
Everson Museum of Art, Syracuse,
New York, Museum Purchase*

Cindy Kolodziejski
Marble Saw Cup, *1989*
Earthenware, 3¾ in. high

The eighteenth century was a period of quickly changing style. Cups were designed in the classical, Rococo, baroque, Empire, Regency, and other styles. Today, however, serious flaws are often apparent in these superficially beautiful objects, which were designed not by potters for practical use but by artists for visual effect. Court painters and sculptors designed their forms without any intimate understanding of the materials or the utilitarian aspects of the cup. Many were created with wide flaring forms to which were attached minute, over-refined handles. The delicate ladies of the times must have had forefingers and thumbs as strong as a heavy-duty vice grip to be able to drink demurely and safely from these unbalanced pieces. What's more, the wide mouths of these cups (influenced in some cases by the design of the Greek kylix) resulted in the tea cooling within minutes of being poured.

The American artist Anne Kraus has created twentieth-century updates of these decorative porcelains. As a painter she was fascinated with the beauty and painterly magnificence of Miessen and Sèvres porcelains but disturbed by the sterility of their beauty: the works had no content or meaning outside their formal esthetic stance. When she was later drawn to ceramics she began to make cups that corrected this

*Late nineteenth-century die-cut
advertisement for Butler's Tea Store,
Amsterdam, New York.*

50

Bolivian
Spanish Colonial Mug,
c. 1870
Etched silver, 3¹⁄₈ in. high

British, Pratt Ware
Bacchus Punch Cup, *c. 1780*
Ceramic, 4¹⁄₈ in. high
Everson Museum of Art, Syracuse,
New York, Gift of Cynthia B. and
Benjamin J. Lake

imbalance, combining the decorative vitality of eighteenth-century wares with modern concerns—alienation, rejection, the desperation and dashed hopes of failure, and unrequited love.

The Populist Cup

Eighteenth-century Britain produced three major technical innovations that profoundly influenced the manufacture of cups and their accessibility to a wider audience. In the second half of the eighteenth century Josiah Wedgwood, the self-styled "potter to the world," perfected the mass production of what was called creamware. Creamware (also known as Queensware) was a finely molded white earthenware with a clear glaze that fired to a distinctive cream color. The efficiency of Wedgwood's production techniques meant that most of Britain's subjects could for the first time afford attractive, immaculately potted tea, coffee, and dinner services. The handsome but now undesirably rough slipwares that most people had owned were banished to rural areas, eventually disappearing almost entirely.

What Wedgwood did for fine earthenware Josiah Spode then did for porcelain. In 1798 he began to produce bone china, a mixture of hard paste porcelain and calcined bone that proved to be suitable for mass

*Late nineteenth-century British
Christmas card.*

Ralph Bacerra
Three Untitled Cups, *1983*
Earthenware with china paint,
3½ in. high

Austrian, Vienna
Tancred Cup and Saucer,
1817
*Porcelain, cup: 4⁵⁄₁₆ in. high,
saucer: 7¹⁄₈ in. diameter
The Metropolitan Museum of Art,
New York, Bequest of
R. Thornton Wilson, 1977*

Miriam Slater
**Gold Playing Card Cup and
Saucer**, *1985*
*Oil and gold leaf on ceramic,
3 in. high*

production. Bone china was not only lighter and more translucent than hard porcelain, but exceedingly durable as well. Within a decade Spode and other British manufacturers were exporting these wares all over the world, and this sophisticated ware now became generally affordable.

At about the same time that Wedgwood was perfecting his creamwares, the use of printed decals or transfers on pottery and porcelain was introduced. This technique, decalcomania, grew out of a craze known as "japanning" that has roots in the seventeenth century. Japanning involved affixing paper engravings, playing cards, and other decorations to metal trays, sealing them with several coats of lacquer, and curing them briefly in a bread oven to harden the surface. The appearance of this ware was not unlike Miriam Slater's *Gold Playing Card Cup and Saucer*, although in this piece the artist has painted the illusion of playing cards sealed under lacquer.

Because the decoration of pottery and porcelain was the most expensive part of the manufacturing process, the ceramics industry had been actively searching for a technique compatible with mass production that would lower this cost. Manufacturers first experimented with stencils, producing work of such skill that it is frequently mistaken for printed decora-

Late nineteenth-century die-cut sticker or seal, manufactured in England.

Staffordshire Potteries, Limited
Cold Coffee Mug, *c. 1982*
Ironstone, 3½ in. high
"Rick must know the truth . . . !,"
laments the text on the other side of
this cup, "(Sob) . . ! The coffee's
cold!"

Roy Lichtenstein
Cups and Saucers from
Rosenthal Tea Service, *1984*
Porcelain, 3 in. high

tion. But the invention of the ceramic transfer or decal opened up new possibilities, and by 1850 experiments began taking place that involved printing transfers on ceramic materials and applying these to the surface of glazed and unglazed wares.

The art of decalcomania was soon perfected, and the presses have never stopped running since. This technique has not only enabled the potter to produce an endless number of pieces with identical scenes or decoration, it has also allowed the cup to become an outspoken propagandist and advertising device. While the commemorative wares of the seventeenth-century slipware potters were relatively costly and could be produced only in limited numbers, transfer printing allowed cups and mugs bearing political, social, or commercial messages to be created in tens of thousands and today by the millions. The printed mug has since become a communications medium of some consequence.

While a detailed examination of political clayware deserves its own study, it is interesting to review some early examples. Illustrated here we find printed mugs and cups ranging from early examples of this technique (see the elegant engraving of the King of Prussia mug) to colorful contemporary cups. The turn-of-century cup that demands "Votes for Women" sported

British, Worcester
Frederick, King of Prussia Mug, *1757*
Ceramic with transfer decoration,
5½ in. high
Everson Museum of Art, Syracuse,
New York, Gift of Cynthia B. and
Benjamin J. Lake
The decal was produced by Robert
Hancock, one of the pioneers of
transfer printing on ceramics.

Villeroy & Boch
Votes for Women, *1909*
Porcelain, 2¾ in. high

Michael Carde·v
Duke Edward for Ever, *1936*
Slipware, 4½ in. high
Cardew, one of the great ceramists
of the twentieth century, produced
mugs with this legend for his
friends, protesting what he saw as
the hypocrisy of Duke Edward's
forced abdication because of his
love for the commoner Mrs.
Wallace Simpson.

an ideally placed message, daily reminding the drinker which sex controlled the teapot and the sensual comforts of domesticity. The cups and mugs of the Russian revolution, however, are among the most dramatic of the propaganda vessels. They were created at two extremes—some artists painted sentimental but moving folk-art renderings that idealized the Soviet worker while others, such as Kazimir Malevich, founder of the suprematist movement, and Nicolai Suetin, produced abstracted, intellectualized, sculptural cups in the avant-garde spirit of the emerging modernist movement. These revolutionary porcelains were not for sale but were displayed in shop windows in larger cities, exhibited as propaganda art to support the fervor and spirit of the new society during its brief flowering of freedom.

A particularly amusing bit of late twentieth-century political commentary takes the form of a commercially produced mug with a three-dollar bill featuring the face of President Richard Nixon. Nixon was not in the least amused when it first came out and had no intention of being "mugged" in this manner. On the tenuous grounds that the manufacturer, General Housewares, had broken a law against reproducing American currency, Nixon sent out teams of Secret Service agents to seize over two thousand of the mugs

General Housewares, Inc.
Three Dollar Mug, *1973*
Earthenware, 3½ in. high

Nicolai Suetin
Suprematist Cup and Saucer,
designed 1923, originally
manufactured by the Petrograd
Porcelain Factory, reproduced for
the Museum of Modern Art by
Mottahdeh, Vista Alegre

Leningrad State Porcelain Factory
Red Faces, 1922
China-painted porcelain,
3⅞ in. high
Elvehjem Museum of Art,
Madison, Wisconsin, lent by
Ludmilla N. Shapiro

Leningrad State Porcelain Factory
**Tenth Anniversary of the
Revolution of 1917**, 1927
Porcelain, 3 in. high
Elvehjem Museum of Art,
Madison, Wisconsin, lent by
Ludmilla N. Shapiro

from wholesalers and retailers. Overnight those that survived this raid became (and have remained) the hottest of Watergate-era collectibles.

The Cup as Victorian Icon

In the late nineteenth century the production of the cup saw only a few innovations, one of which was the Victorian moustache cup. This vessel had an internal shelf that held the drinker's moustache above the liquid so that he could enjoy his beverage without getting a soggy upper lip—a dubious-sounding design that did actually work but never gained much popularity. Overall, this was a stylistically anarchic period of mix-and-match revivalist ideas that produced some of the most excessive overdecoration in the history of man. Around this time a series of reformist design movements began, the central and most important of which was the Arts and Crafts Movement, which produced simpler designs with a greater commitment to what was known as "truth to materials." The simplicity injected in late nineteenth-century design by reformers, however, did not undercut the popularity of commemorative wares, the favorite subject of which has traditionally been royalty. Ever since Queen Victoria's reign, the manufacture of cups commemorating the British royal family has thrived among armies of loyal

Betty Woodman and Viola Frey
Collaboration Cup, 1987
*Porcelain with china paint,
3¾ in. high*

Late nineteenth-century die-cut cup stickers or seals sporting affectionate mottos, manufactured in England.

This late Victorian card, produced around 1895, is hinged so that the cup pivots up to reveal a fortune or greeting. The fad of reading one's fortune in tea leaves lasted until World War II and, though much less popular, continues today.

Your fortunes in the tea-cup,
You will see—just lift it up!

St. Valentine's Greeting.

Absent but dear

Forget me not.

True Love.

Faithfulness

French
Mug, *c. 1898*
Glass cup in silver stand, 3 in. high

Pietro Krohn, Bing & Grondahl
Porcelain Factory
Cup from Heron Service, *1888*
Porcelain, 3 in. high
Bing & Grondahl Porcelain
Factory, Copenhagen

William Moorcroft, McIntyre
Pottery
Florian Ware Loving Cup, *1902*
Ceramic, 7¹/₁₆ in. high
Private collection

Postmarked July 26, 1906, this card is a quirky mixture of Gothic and Jugenstil design.

collectors. Much like medieval cups, these wares celebrate coronations, marriages, and births, and, at times, mourn deaths. While most are intended to reflect a sense of dignity and reverence, several clever satirical pieces have also been created. One of the best is a recent commercially manufactured mug that makes the most of Prince Charles's regal ears, giving his portrait mug generous and appropriate handles.

Wilkinson Pottery
Royal Commemorative Cups,
1937
Earthenware with printed
decoration, 4 and 5 in. high
Private collection

Carlton Ware
Charles Charming, 1981
Ceramic, 3½ in. high
Prince Charles's famous ears make
for this amusing play on the "ear"
of a cup, as its handle is
often known.

This postcard from 1977 gently
satirizes Queen Elizabeth II and
Prince Philip, whose likenesses
drink here from commemorative
ware. Illustration by Roger Law
and Peter Fluck.

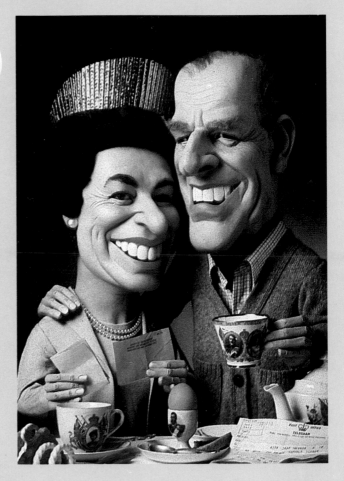

Laura Lasworth
Lorain Throws a Cup, *1983*
Acrylic on masonite, 12 in. high

Amy Sabrina
Self-Portrait, *1989*
Earthenware, 3½ in. high

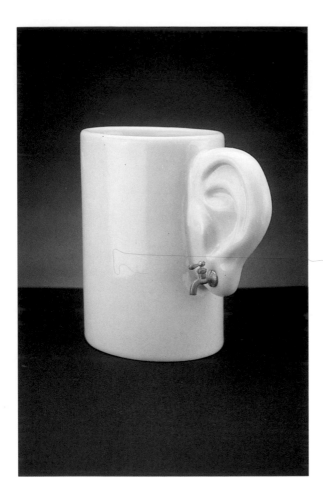

Marc Farrington
Robot Cup, 1985
Earthenware, 3½ in. high

Natasha Nicholson,
Sunshine Ceramics
Ear Cup with Faucet, 1983
Earthenware, 3⅝ in. high

Signed AA/NYC
Faucet Cup, 1978
Ceramic, 4 in. high

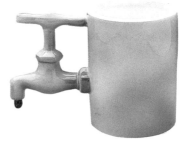

The cup in the late 1800s became a very popular and highly commercialized icon owing to the increased popularity of tea drinking and because of the aura of home and hearth that the cup suggested. It became one of the most popular themes for postcard manufacturers and advertisers, somewhat inexplicably used to offer birthday greetings, Valentine's Day affections, Christmas cheer, get-well wishes, and just about every other kind of sentiment.

Die-cut advertisements in the shape of cups were particularly popular and used more appropriately by tea and coffee importers although they were also strange favorites with hardware store owners and makers of building materials. Among the more complex of these cards were those that dealt with the turn-of-the-century vogue for reading fortunes through tea leaves. The cups on these cards had pockets containing detailed guides on how to read the tea leaves. This design survived up until the 1950s when the introduction of the pragmatic and unromantic tea bag laid this fad to rest.

The symbolic use of the cup has continued into the present day and still serves as the universal sign for refreshment, as can be seen in millions of coffee and tea shop signs all over the world. One of the most evocative of these signs was captured by the American photogra-

Karen Koblitz
Betty's Cup, *1982*
Earthenware, 9 × 8½ in.

German or Austrian card, c. 1905.

Phillip Maberry
Cup, 1986
Porcelain, 2⅝ in. high

73

pher Edward Weston in 1937. Standing in the blistering heat of the Mohave Desert is a forlorn and weathered sign offering the dubious relief of hot coffee.

Art Meets Life in the Modern Cup

The twentieth century has produced many new styles from art nouveau to art deco, from modernism to postmodernism. But what is special about the cup in the twentieth century has been the emergence of the "art" cup. While fine artists in previous centuries had designed functional cups, in the twentieth century purely decorative cups were first created. Modern artists approach the cup as a primary format for expression. Malevich's half-cup is a good early example of this sculptural direction. But perhaps the most powerful art cup to emerge from early modernism is Meret Oppenheim's fur teacup, a masterpiece of the surrealist movement. This provocative cup transforms the object's natural suggestion of intimacy and pleasurable tactile qualities into a nightmarish creation that repels both one's mind and one's lips.

Then there are cups that artists have created to confuse rather than to repel. Marilyn Levine's "leather" and "denim" cups are a good case in point.

Kazimir Malevich,
Leningrad State Porcelain Factory
Half Cup, *1920*
Porcelain, 2½ in. high
Elvehjem Museum of Art,
Madison, Wisconsin, lent by
Ludmilla N. Shapiro

Paul Mathieu
This Is Not a Cup, *1988*
Porcelain, 9 in. diameter

Wassily Kandinsky,
Haviland et Cie
Cup and Saucer,
designed c. 1920, produced 1972
Ceramic, 2⅝ in. high

Akio Takamori
Male and Female Cups, *1985*
Slip and glaze on stoneware, male:
6¾ in. high, female: 6 in. high

Miriam Slater
Leopard Cup and Saucer,
1986
Painted ceramic, 2¼ in. high

Meret Oppenheim
**Souvenir du Déjeuner en
Fourrure**, *1936*
Cloth, fur, glass, wood, 6 in. high

Below:
Meret Oppenheim
Objet, *1936*
Fur-covered cup, 4 in. high
Museum of Modern Art, New York

David Furman
Faber Castell Cup, *1987*
Ceramic with ceramic crayons and
paint, 3 in. high

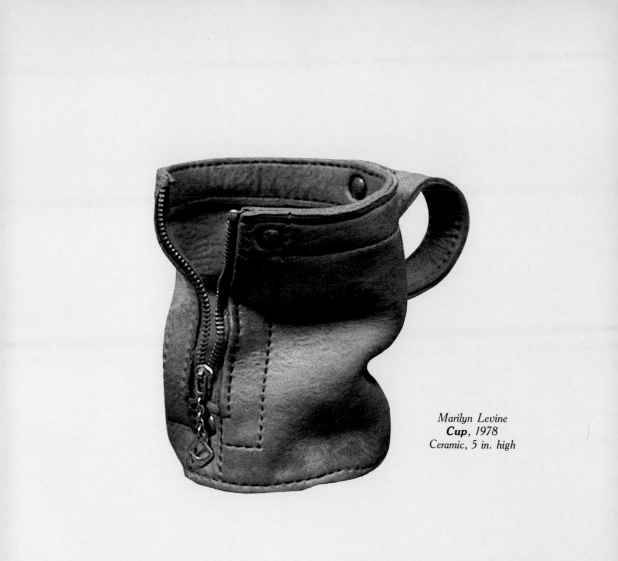

Marilyn Levine
Cup, *1978*
Ceramic, 5 in. high

Levine's leather- or denimlike surfaces in stoneware are so convincing that only by touching them is one made aware that things are not what they seem to be. This trompe l'oeil tradition of deception is also employed in Richard Shaw's *Rope Cup* and in Nancy Selvin's *Tin Can Cup*.

Richard Notkin's cups are concerned not with the superrealism of pop art but rather with realism in its more traditional context, linked to the social activism of the so-called "Trashcan" school of American painters in the 1930s. There is a tenderness about the manner in which Notkin creates cups out of our society's garbage—discarded tires, barrels, broken building blocks, dented trashcans, and empty packing cases—but at the same time, Notkin issues a judgment, a softly delivered rebuke about the manner in which our culture consumes and pollutes.

Some artists are attracted to the cup because of its banality. This in part is what makes the cup such a powerful motif for pop artists. Oldenburg, known for his sculptures of clothespins, telephones, toilets, and other household objects, made soft, gestural cups out of plaster and also created a memorable print in which a cup was drawn with coffee stains. Roy Lichtenstein's cups, on the other hand, are formal plays on the nature of three-dimensional and two-dimensional realities.

Jerry Walberg
Untitled Cups with Shorts,
1969
Stoneware, 4¾ in. high

William Wilhelmi
Cowboy Boot Cup, *1984*
Porcelain, 5½ in. high

Amy Sabrina
Cup Quilt, *1984*
Cotton, *80 × 80 in.*

Richard Notkin
Wooden Crate Cup, 1982
Stoneware, 4 in. high

Nancy Selvin
Tin Can Cup, 1980
Earthenware, 2⅝ in. high

Richard Shaw
**Cast Rope Cup with Knife
Handle**, 1970
Earthenware with china paint,
4 in. high

Richard Notkin
Barrel Cup with Tire, 1975
Ceramic and china paint,
2¾ in. high

83

His pieces are decorated with shadows, highlights, and reflections that one might ordinarily expect to see on the surface of a glossy object, although this illusion of light and shade comes not from nature but from the graphic pattern on the cup's surface.

While pop artists have delighted in the cup's ordinariness, other artists have been attracted to the cup for its scale. Kenneth Price has worked with the form throughout his career. His geometric cups of the early 1970s were small masterpieces of contemporary art, amalgams of art deco, cubism, and the fetish-finish school of Southern California art. Price's colorful *Cubist Cup* deals not only with the cup but with its unseen spatial milieu, defining the way in which a cup conceptually occupies space by outlining this perceived territory with brightly colored geometric appendages. American artist Ron Nagle has made a virtual career out of this idea, producing small-scaled, precious, but powerful works in which the function of the cup has become irrelevant, which in turn reduces the cup to purely formal exploration of its two elements—handle and vessel.

A small-scale object such as a cup can have surprising strength. It can also present what British potter and miniaturist Geoffrey Swindell calls "the unexpectedness of scale." In Marilyn Lysohir's antiwar state-

Claes Oldenburg
Coffee Cup, *1973*
Lithograph on paper,
18 × 23½ in.

Claes Oldenburg
Coffee Cup, *1962*
Plaster and enamel paint,
6 in. high

Kenneth Price
Cubist Cup, 1973
Porcelain, 3½ in. high

Lidya Buzio
Cityscape Cups, 1984
Burnished earthenware,
4¾ and 5 in. high

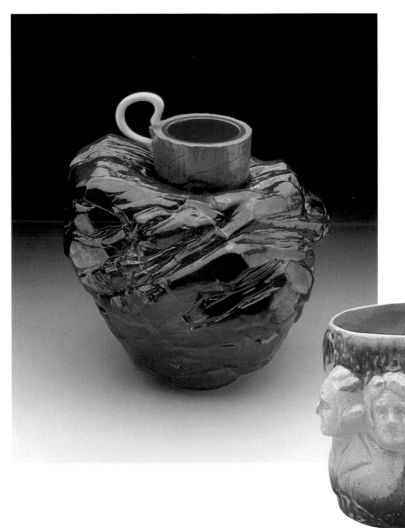

Anthony Bennett
Cup with Rock Saucer, *1986*
Earthenware, 8½ in. high

Black Hills Clay
**Mount Rushmore National
Memorial, Black Hills,
South Dakota**, *c. 1960*
Ceramic, 4 in. high

Carol McNicol
Large Cup, 1971
Earthenware, 36 in. diameter
Private collection

Ann Wolff
Cup and Saucer, 1982
Handblown glass, 4½ in. high

ment *Dazzle Cup and Saucer*, we are surprised to find only upon close examination a tiny battleship floating in a sea of coffee. But scale can work in two ways. British artist Carol McNicol quadrupled the normal scale of the cup for her *Large Cup*, whose thirty-six-inch diameter cup and saucer produces a sense of gigantism despite the fact that thirty-six inches is actually rather small in sculptural terms. Anna Silver works with the same distortion of normalcy in her giant, skillfully painted, Disney-like cups, which would be perfectly at home at the most surreal mad hatter's tea parties.

I leave this essay with a plea on behalf of the cup. In his book *Ceramics* (1984), Philip Rawson warns that our culture faces the danger of suffering what he chillingly describes as "tactile castration" because we are no longer conscious of the feel and sensuality of everyday objects. Ironically, one of the last cups featured in this book is a ceramic rendering by Victor Spinski of the most popularly used cup of the twentieth century, the Styrofoam mug. This vessel, with its dry puckered surface, is what modern man reaches for most often when seeking refreshment.

Edie Ellis
Untitled, *1987*
Blue glitter on glass, 3 in. high

Postcard from the early 1980s.

With this in mind, could we not consider replacing our bland mugs bearing corporate logos, personal names, or dull advertisements with something a touch more fanciful? Perhaps a cup that expresses a sense of humor, a political, spiritual, or artistic viewpoint. After all, few objects occupy as special a place in our daily lives. We experience the cup with the casual intimacy of lovers, lip to lip. We should pause and sensually enjoy the refinement of the cup's materials, the silkiness of its glaze, its rich and warming feel. The lowly cup can surprise, and remind us that the greatest exoticism might be right in our hands in the commonplace.

Victor Spinski
Spilled Coffee, *1978*
Ceramic, 3¾ in. high

Acknowledgments

Despite the compact nature of this book many individuals have contributed to its creation, and I am most grateful for their participation. Wayne Kuwada has assisted with many aspects of the photography including the elegant styling of the setups. My partner Mark Del Vecchio has, as always, been a source of support and encouragement, taking up the slack in my absence at the gallery. Tony Cunha has been responsible for almost all of the photography in this book and has worked on this project with his usual skill, perceptiveness, and good humor. My thanks also to the Cooper-Hewitt Museum, the Metropolitan Museum, the Everson Museum, and the Nelson-Atkins Museum for their assistance. At Abbeville Press, Sharon Gallagher helped form this project with her incisive pragmatism, for which I am grateful. My editor Constance Herndon's belief kept our enthusiasm alive, and her judicious blue pencil and imaginative suggestions have been crucial to many of this little book's strengths. My thanks also to the book's designer Molly Shields for her graphic transformations.

Lastly, I would like to offer my thanks to Betty Asher, not just for working so tirelessly with me on *The Book of Cups* but also for a valued friendship and for shared passion in the humble cup.

Index Page numbers in *italics* refer to illustrations.

Photo Credits

All photography by Tony Cunha unless otherwise credited in
the captions, with the exception of the images on pages 18 and
35, courtesy of the Bettman Archive, New York, and that on
page 90, courtesy of Philip-Dimitri Galas/Galas Exoticards,
San Diego.

About the Author and Photographer

Garth Clark is the author of eleven books and over one hundred essays, reviews, and articles on ceramics. Recipient of the 1980 Art Critics Award from the National Endowment for the Arts, Clark is also the director of two contemporary ceramics galleries, in New York and Los Angeles, and lectures widely throughout the U.S. and Europe. His most recent books include *The Eccentric Teapot* (1989), *The Mad Potter of Biloxi: The Art and Life of George E. Ohr* (1989), and *American Ceramics: 1876 to the Present* (1988), all published by Abbeville.

Tony Cunha is a Los Angeles–based photographer whose work includes both commercial and art photography. He was educated at the Art Center College of Design in California, and his images have been published in art, architecture, and interior design magazines in the United States and Europe.

Don Schreckengost, Salem Pottery
Tricorne Cup, *c. 1940*
Ceramic, 3¼ in. high